"They Promoted Me?"

"They Promoted Me?"

A Primer For The New Supervisor

by

Jim Weaver

toExcel

San Jose · New York · Lincoln · Shanghai

"They Promoted Me?"
A Primer For The New Supervisor

This edition published by toExcel Press,
an imprint of iUniverse.com, Inc.

For information address:
iUniverse.com, Inc.
620 North 48th Street
Suite 201
Lincoln, NE 68504-3467
www.iUniverse.com

ISBN: 1-58348-737-9

Printed in the United States of America

PREFACE

So, you finally got promoted. Congratulations! You've probably spent hours studying for exams, preparing for oral boards, or maybe even participating in some type of assessment center. You came out on top and have reached your dream of becoming a supervisor.

Unfortunately, getting promoted no more makes you a supervisor than walking into an airport makes you a pilot. Organizations are renown for creating intricate, complex, supervisory selection processes, then following them up with absolutely no supervisory training whatsoever. Consequently, the new supervisor is left to twist in the organizational wind with little more to guide him/her than the internal compass which has pointed the way thus far. That constitutes a problem, and here's why.

Political appointments aside, most workers who reach the rank of "supervisor" were, before that, "super doers." That is, they came to work, did their job, did it well, and impressed their bosses. When the time came to compete for a supervisory rank, they engaged the task with relish, beat out the competition, and, as one would have predicted, got themselves promoted. Now, with no specialized supervisory training, they approach the task of supervision with the same enthusiasm they had as a worker. Unfortunately, they will now be evaluated not on what they do, but rather on what they are able to get subordinates to do…two totally different tasks.

It is not only unfair, it is unreasonable to expect that someone can supervise well simply because he/she has been promoted. This assumption is proven over and over by listening to the complaints of subordinates who suffer under the oversight of a well-intended, but poorly trained supervisor.

That's why this primer was written. It is designed to be a succinct collection of common sense principles and techniques to help the new supervisor get off and running down the track without stumbling out of the blocks. If you are a worker who is dealing with a newly promoted but woefully under-trained supervisor, buy him/her this book. It may well be the best thing you ever did...for yourself and your organization.

ACKNOWLEDGEMENTS

I would like to express my sincere appreciation to Ray Weaver for his great editorial skill, and manuscript enhancement efforts. Pam Weaver and Molly LaGatta invested many hours and much energy into proofreading and polishing the initial and final drafts. Without the dedication of these three people, this work would not have become a reality. My wife, Karin, offered new ideas and the continual support which helped me remain focused. For that, I will always be appreciative. Finally, I would like to thank the long list of mentors who came before me, and contributed to my own supervisory education. You know who you are. To all of you, my heartfelt thanks.

CONTENTS

I

The View Only Changes For The Lead Dog
Keeping Your Promotion In Perspective

Check your ego at the door. You're happy you got promoted, and your family is happy you got promoted. That about sums it up. The person who promoted you must now face those who didn't get promoted. Superiors in the chain of command higher than you couldn't really care less, and as far as your old co-workers are concerned, their view from the cheap seats changes very little. So strut like a peacock for a day or so, then get your nose out of the air and down to the grindstone.

As the old cliché atones, "Rome wasn't built in a day." Now before you say, "that's because I wasn't in charge," remember this: change is traumatic—for those who implement it, and especially for those who must adapt to it. If you see your new supervisory role as that of a change agent, gauge your speed, then back it down about six notches. Most organizations, even those in need of vast improvement, will not react positively to any changes, especially radical, rapid dictates from the "new boss."

Your new subordinates will need time to adjust to you in your new position. You may look different, you certainly belong to a new level in the chain of command, and eventually you will learn to think and act differently than your subordinates. You now carry the big management stick. However, any abrupt attempt to swing it, will be perceived as aggressive and intimidating by those around you. Take Teddy's advice and walk softly at first. As you will see in Chapter Two, your role must indeed change, but proceed slowly and cautiously at first.

It is almost impossible to receive a promotion to supervisor without sensing a new aura of pride and an elevation in your self-esteem. However, you must be careful not to allow this positive "look what I did" attitude to deteriorate into a condescending approach toward others. This is especially difficult because there are those in the organization who will immediately begin to ingratiate themselves to you. Don't be fooled. You're no prettier, no smarter, and no more charismatic than you were yesterday. But today you're a supervisor, and these "brownnosers" will say and do anything if they think you might be able to do something for them in your new supervisory role.

What's more, you must be on guard against those who would like to sink your ship very early. True, only a few are delighted with your promotion, and most don't care. But there are always some who are jealous or feel cheated because you made it and they didn't. It may not happen immediately, but these self-serving simpletons will attempt to feel better about themselves by creating subterfuge and placing booby traps in your path. You can't tell who they are by looking at them, and most are clever as a fox. The best way to avoid embarrassment at their hands is to weigh every bit of input you receive in light of your new position as supervisor.

Finally, you must understand that this new credibility you are experiencing by virtue of being promoted is fragile and will be short-lived if you don't begin to act like a supervisor. In effect, you've been placed on stage, and everyone is watching to see if you can dance.

It is a virtual tightrope which requires you to establish a direction, and proceed smoothly (not run) along a path of accomplishment as opposed to knee jerk actions. At your own behest, the ball is now in your court. The question becomes, "What are you going to do with it?"

What Did He Just Say?

Don't

1) Don't let your promotion go to your head. Plenty got promoted before you, and plenty will after.
2) Don't go crazy implementing a bunch of radical changes. Allow your subordinates to get used to you.
3) Don't magically change into a totally different person with new values and opinions.

Do

1) Be aware of those who view your promotion as a chance to use it for their own personal gain.
2) Be on guard against those who would seek to sabotage you in your new rank.
3) Get off the dime and do something supervisory. This will give your subordinates confidence in your ability.

II

What Do I Do Now?
Realizing Your New Role

Have you ever heard the expression, "Yesterday ended last night"? Well, guess what? So did your career; or at least what used to be your career. Ready or not, the minute you were awarded your promotion, your old role ceased to exist, and your new role began. Never again will you be just one of the guys. Never again will co-workers (now subordinates) freely express their thoughts without considering the ramifications of saying something improper or in the wrong way to you, the supervisor. Never again will you be able to poke fun at someone of a lesser rank without suffering criticism for humiliating a subordinate. Never again will you be able to play favorites because you like one person better than another. Never again will you be able to grouse about management, because you're now expected to be part of the solution rather than the problem.

Most people who are promoted understand that things will be different, but they seldom realize the dramatic shift that occurs immediately after they accept the position of supervisor. In some instances where the new supervisor had been socially active in the workplace, he/she may even sense a feeling of loneliness when ostracized from the coffee break patter, luncheon outings, and happy hour excursions, which by design, occur without supervisors. Sorry, but it goes with the territory. Just as movie stars lose their privacy, new supervisors lose their distinction as one of the guys. There are several reasons why it must be this way.

Initially, you now have a form of power not available to the average worker. It is called "legitimate power," and it derives from the fact that you are assigned a certain level of authority by the organization simply by virtue of your new rank. You may now evaluate, counsel, reward, discipline, and give direct orders. You have a more sophisticated job description, a new level of liberty, and a voice which speaks for others in addition to yourself.

Secondly, your appearance is now different. By virtue of stripes on your sleeve, gold on your badge, or the word "Supervisor" on your shirt, you announce to everyone who sees you that you are something above and beyond the average worker. In paramilitary organizations you are no longer called by your name. Instead, you are addressed by your rank. Without saying a word, you now intimidate people you once considered to be your peers and associates. Because you will be the one to evaluate their performance, they see you as someone who can help and/or hinder their own career. Therefore, they will go to great extremes to put the most positive spin on everything about them that comes to your attention.

Finally, you will eventually evolve into a different type of employee. Supervision, regardless of the type of organization, is considered to be the first rung of the management ladder. As such, you will be more exposed to management thinking relative to goals, objectives, vision, and focus of the organization. You will be expected to embrace those philosophies and to espouse them to your subordinates. As a result, you will develop a keener insight into the organizational climate; and you will eventually become a supportive member of the management culture.

One of the most difficult role changes which must occur with the first line supervisor is to make the transition from the one who actually does the work to the one who now oversees others who do the work. A major frustration at this juncture occurs because you as a supervisor must now deal with workers in the organization who are complacent, mediocre, and disinterested in doing their jobs. They are, in fact, just the opposite of how you were before you became a supervisor. That is not to say they aren't busy. In fact, you will notice early on that they work just as hard (or harder) to keep from doing the job as they would if they simply did what was expected of them. And to make matters worse, you will seldom be permitted to solve the problem by transfer or termination of the employee. You must, in fact, figure out a way to propel them to a higher level of productivity—an often complex and labor intensive endeavor. You will have to resist the urge to give up and reassign the task, or finish it yourself. It might be easier, but that is not what supervisors do. It is this very complex supervisory problem which will haunt you throughout your remaining supervisory years.

Finally, you will notice that your job has become hectic and full of interruptions. The reason is because you are now solving problems for five or seven or fifteen as opposed to just one. You will seldom get one problem solved before two more emerge. Although you no longer do the actual work, you will constantly be working close to the people you supervise. You will find the hours of the workday pass very quickly as you make assignments, observe work activity, initiate adjustments and corrections, encounter employee problems, carry out management dictates, and deal with unhappy customers. More than once, you'll mentally ask, "How did I ever get myself into this mess?"

What Did He Just Say?

Don't

1) Don't expect life to be the same after promotion. It changes quickly and drastically.
2) Don't take it personally if your old peers seem to cut you out of the social loop. It comes with being the boss.
3) Don't abuse your newly found power and liberty. Both carry with them a high level of responsibility for their use.

Do

1) Learn to enjoy your new role in the organization. With a little time, your comfort level will increase measurably.
2) Challenge yourself to deal effectively with unmotivated employees. Try new ideas, and don't get frustrated by this age-old problem.
3) Work to understand the new management concepts to which you are exposed. Participate in all workplace management sessions to which you are invited. The knowledge you will gain is invaluable.

III

Anybody Got A Road Map?
Learning The Goals Of Your Organization

A famous French naturalist did an experiment with processionary caterpillars.Processionary caterpillars are so named because of their proclivity to follow each other around in parade fashion. He placed the caterpillars on a large table, forming them head to tail into a circle. True to form, they began to follow each other around and around. At the end of the third day, the naturalist placed some pine needles, the caterpillars favorite food, into the middle of the circle. Although they were hungry, and their favorite food was only inches away, they continued to follow each other around and around until, by the end of the seventh day, they had all perished from starvation and exhaustion. Why? Because they were "activity oriented" instead of "accomplishment oriented."

The two are not the same. Any organization worth its salt has a vision, an idea of where it wants to go. It then develops goals and objectives, the conceptual vehicles to get them there. Without goals and objectives, an organization is no better than a ship without a rudder, hopelessly tossed to and fro with no particular port as a target. Admittedly, some organizations do a poor job of communicating their ambitions down the chain of command. Consequently, organizational movement becomes "activity oriented" as opposed to "accomplishment oriented." Regardless, one of your early responsibilities as a new supervisor will be to learn both the goals of your organization (what it is trying to accomplish) and the objectives of your organization (how is it trying to accomplish those goals).

You are going to become very busy very quickly. Provided the goals and objectives are adequately entrenched in the back of your mind, you will always be cognizant of the direction you are heading and will parallel the direction of the organization. Without this knowledge, you will waste unnecessary energy and will, like the caterpillars, end up exactly where you started—exhausted and having accomplished nothing particularly meaningful.

What's more, your subordinates will work more productively if they understand the overall mission of the organization. Psychologists say that at some point in time, employees must be able to stand back, assess their work product, and find value in the job they perform. Absent meaningful objectives, it is impossible for them to determine their level of success. Several years ago, I took over a unit where the employees were indeed busy and in some respects were doing a pretty decent job. The problem was that they had no idea of the organizational goals, and had never articulated a set of measurable objectives which would support those goals. As their new supervisor, I immediately set up an off-site training session and introduced them to the concept of goals and objectives. I then assisted them with the development of their individual objectives and required them to predict in round numbers what they expected to accomplish during each quarter of the fiscal year. In the beginning, they were extremely uncomfortable with this new level of expectation. However, by the end of the first quarter, when they actually saw what they had accomplished as a team with a new direction, their level of self-esteem and job satisfaction soared. They either matched or exceeded every objective for the remainder of the year. Benchmarks, which allow the employee to measure success, along with reinforcement by you for successful performance, will ensure that your subordinates remain happy and enthusiastic as they pursue their daily work activities.

Finally, an accurate understanding of your organization's goals will help you prepare for higher levels of management responsibility down the road. By working with goals at this early stage in your supervisory/management life, you become comfortable with the performance expectations which accompany those goals. Further, experience working in a goal-oriented atmosphere lends itself well when the time comes for you to assist in the creation of new visions and goals.

What Did He Just Say?

Don't

1) Don't confuse being busy with being productive. Many workers stay very busy but accomplish little.

2) Don't assume your subordinates know about goals and objectives. Without training, they automatically work in a reactive mode.

3) Don't wait for your supervisor to train you in the goals of your organization. Take active steps to learn them on your own.

Do

1) Make sure that the things you are doing with your subordinates are in support of the organizational goals.

2) Train your subordinates in organizational direction. Help them to develop specific, measurable, attainable, and time-phased objectives related to the organizational goals.

3) Get comfortable with the "goals and objectives" concept as soon as possible. Use it to train yourself for the future.

IV

Subordinates From Hell
Understanding Your Employees

I once had a neighbor who was a dog trainer. He always said that there were two ways to train a dog. One was to beat him into submission. The other was to persuade him that it was in both their best interests for the dog to do what the trainer wanted. Both ways worked. But the first method resulted in a terrorized animal that obeyed begrudgingly and out of fear. The second method produced a happy, talented animal that obeyed his trainer out of love and respect.

Your subordinates are not animals, but the illustration remains valid. You have the power as their supervisor to gain compliance through fear and intimidation, or to persuade them that it is in both your best interests to do what you want them to do.

In many respects, training the dogs might be easier. In order for a dogsled to make progress, all the Huskies must be pulling in the same direction. But if you understand the mind-set of one Husky, you pretty much understand them all. They all think and act in about the same manner. People are very much different. Each has his/her own mind set, motivation, and behavior patterns which may or may not reflect that of others in the same work group.

So the question becomes, "How do you, as the supervisor, get a group of very different people all pulling together to advance the sled in the same direction?" An initial important step is to understand some basic concepts about employees in general.

First, most employees don't come to work just to get a paycheck. Obviously the pay is important, and they wouldn't come anymore if the organization stopped paying them; but, paychecks are like heartbeats. People don't think much about them until they stop. Most employees see work as a social activity...a chance to interact with other employees on both a personal and professional basis. So important is this activity that some employees go a bit stir-crazy after retirement unless they maintain an activity which allows a form of social interaction to continue.

Secondly, not every employee engages in work with the same level of enthusiasm and energy. Any expectation on your part that a ten-year veteran will embrace his/her responsibilities with the same fervor of a brand new employee is unreasonable. We are talking plowhorses versus racehorses here. Is one better than the other? Not necessarily. The veteran may move a little more slowly, but he/she knows the system, understands the mission, and can be expected over the long haul to do what is expected. The new employee has the fire, the zeal, and the eagerness to please. However, he/she will probably make frequent mistakes and require admonition and guidance during the initial job learning curve period. Understanding this about your subordinates allows you the opportunity to shift supervisory gears based on your knowledge of the employees.

Thirdly, employees are dynamic. That means they change throughout their career due to events which impact them both on and off the job. New employees may enter the workplace enthusiastically, ready to save the world, and intent upon climbing to the top of the executive ladder. But after a couple of years on the job, when they realize they are not going to make the difference they thought they could, or feel that the organization doesn't appreciate their contribution as much as they thought it should, the employee's mind-set changes. Further, personal problems, be they marital, financial, parental, or whatever, divert the employee's concentration away from work-related responsibilities. In most instances, the employee eventually recovers and continues to contribute, but this state of constant flux is an element the supervisor must factor into his/her equation about what makes the employee tick.

Finally, every employee has a "button" which, when identified and pushed by the supervisor, can result in better employee performance. We are not talking about manipulation here, but rather an effective supervisory tool. Although we will address motivation in more detail later, it is important for you to know that, once again, the trigger which stimulates one subordinate, is probably not going to work for another. It therefore becomes imperative for you as the new supervisor to meet with each employee, one on one, and invest the time to learn about each of them as individuals. You can't accomplish this with one formal meeting, but it is a good place to start. Once completed, you must continue to be employee-oriented. The higher one rises in the management ranks, the more removed he/she becomes from the employees who do the work. At the higher management levels this is both acceptable and appropriate. But at the supervisory level, you must remain in constant contact with the people who work for you. The supervisor who remains aloof and distant will, in short term, lose touch and become ineffective.

What Did He Just Say?

Don't

1) Don't expect your subordinates to be the same. They are unique individuals with different mind-sets and different motivations.
2) Don't restrict normal social interaction in the workplace. It is necessary and promotes productivity.
3) Don't try to supervise from a distance. Effective supervision is accomplished by staying close to the subordinates.

Do

1) Set out immediately to understand your subordinates. They will love to tell you about themselves if you give them the chance.
2) Learn what makes each employee tick, and modify your motivational technique as necessary.
3) Remain flexible when your subordinates experience personal and/or professional setbacks. Be supportive and less demanding during times of trouble.

V

Do What I Mean, Not What I Say
Communicating With Your Employees

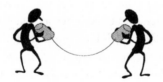

A restaurant owner ordered 400 hams for the Easter season restaurant special. A few weeks before Easter, however, reservations were disappointingly slow. Worried that he might not secure the required number of seatings, he called the distributor and instructed him to, "Cut my order in half!"

When his order arrived, guess what it contained? 400 hams, of course, each cut in half! Did the distributor do what he was told? Absolutely. Did the restaurant owner get what he wanted? Nope. Why? Because the distributor heard what the restaurant owner said, but not what he meant.

Mark my word, and take this to the bank. If communication isn't clear, productivity always suffers. If you as a new supervisor do not say what you mean, mean what you say, and ensure that your subordinate completely understands what you are communicating, you will not get the results you want. I would even go so far as to say that communication is the skill you will use most in the workplace. Therefore, you need to invest the energy necessary to develop it to its highest possible level.

Entire books have been devoted to the skill of communication. It is not within the scope of this primer to analyze every aspect of the skill. The basic tenets remain constant, however, and are very important to you as a supervisor.

If you want your subordinates to do something, you must tell them what it is you want...not in nebulous, ethereal terms, but with specific, simple, definable, clear instructions. No one is a mind reader. If you don't tell them what you want, they'll never be able to guess. What is even more frustrating, however, is that they will seldom petition you for clarification. Children will—adults will not. Remember in the movie *Coming To America*, Eddie Murphy arrives in Queens and takes a low-level job in a fast-food restaurant. The owner gives him a mop, which is standing in a mop bucket on wheels and says, "You do know how to mop a floor, don't you?" Eddie Murphy says, "Oh, yes." Then he begins to roll the bucket around the floor without ever taking the mop out. He had no idea what to do, but he didn't want to ask the owner for fear of looking dumb. The point is this: You must tell your subordinates what you want them to do. Then you must query them to insure that they understand your directions. In other words, some feedback mechanism must exist which allows you to know from the very beginning that the employee understands your intent. It can be as simple as, "O.K. Tell me what you think I want you to do." Have them parrot the instructions back. You will know immediately if you were clearly understood. Never be satisfied with asking, "Do you understand what I want?" Because the answer will always be, "Yes" regardless of whether they understand or not.

Never attempt to communicate when you are in a highly emotional state. Remember, most of your subordinates are somewhat intimidated by your position, and others are downright frightened. As a result, the things you say may be skewed, or even masked by the manner in which you say them. I have always prided myself in being a "people person," and have tried not to act like what you might call a "highbrow" communicator. I would never say something like, "If you do so-and-so again, I will be forced to take retributive action." One time, however, in a state of frustration, I told a subordinate named Bill, "If you do that again, I'll break all the fingers on your right hand." Over the next several days, I noticed that Bill, who was usually a very social guy, appeared somewhat cool to me. In talking with another subordinate, I mentioned the change I'd noticed in him. She responded by saying, "Oh, he thinks you don't like him." Stunned, I asked, "Why?" She said, "Did you threaten to hurt him? He said you threatened to break his fingers." I was absolutely dumbfounded. I said, "Yes, I said it; but I was only joking. How could someone take that seriously?" She said, "I don't know, but Bill did. Maybe you should clear it up with him." I did. And from that point forward, I became very aware of emotions, and how they can become a barrier to effective communication. I hadn't been angry with Bill, but he had perceived it that way. And that made it real. I also became more careful about the way I spoke to my subordinates. I learned the hard way that it wasn't always going to be understood in the way I intended.

In addition to speaking properly and clearly, another major form of communication is the skill of listening. You will make as big an impact on your subordinates by listening as you ever will by talking. In fact, research shows that almost one-half of your workday will be spent listening to someone talk to you about something. As the boss, you must articulate your wishes. But you demonstrate concern for your subordinates by listening to them, not talking to them. The caveat of listening is that you listen at a rate which is much faster than the person who is talking speaks. As a result, it is not uncommon for your mind to begin to wander while you're supposed to be listening. In order to minimize this, you should try to listen "actively." That is, organize, summarize, and review what is being said to you. If appropriate, stop and paraphrase the things you are hearing. Not only will it help you pay attention to the message, but you might even learn something. It is also important to maintain eye contact with the person who is communicating with you. It is a very common assumption that if you are not looking, you're not listening. People are very conscious of this. If you don't believe it, try this little experiment. Next time someone is talking to you, take your eyes off him or her, lift your wrist, look at your watch, then look back at them. You will cause them to completely lose their train of thought. Nine times out of ten, they will ask if you have to be some place, or if you are late for something. You will have to reassure them that you are still willing to continue listening...if, in fact, you are.

Finally, one of the most important supervisory communicative techniques I have ever discovered is the art of asking questions. It has been my experience that subordinates who almost never volunteer information are perfectly willing to answer questions as long as you are willing to ask. A friend of mine once paid my boss a nice compliment. They had met during the social hour at a professional convention. His compliment went something like this. "He is an excellent conversationalist. I thoroughly enjoyed talking with him." A few weeks later, I heard the same compliment again from a totally different person. So I started paying attention to my boss's interactions during social and professional activities. It wasn't long before I discovered his secret. All he did was ask questions. He gave people a chance to talk about themselves, and they liked him for it. When I queried him about it sometime later, he responded, "People don't care about you until you show them you care about them. And besides, I've never learned anything when my mouth was open."

You can learn about budgets; you can be a time management wizard; you can memorize rules and regulations; and write meticulous policies and procedures. You can look the part, and wear the stripes as proudly as anyone else. But the bottom line, and the fact of the matter, is that if you can't communicate, you can't supervise. There is no skill which will take its place, and no trick in your bag that is more valuable.

What Did He Just Say?

Don't

1) Don't assume that your subordinates understand what you said. Use the technique of paraphrasing to insure understanding.

2) Don't expect your employees to ask for clarification. They don't want to ask what might be perceived as a dumb question.

3) Be careful with the use of your words. Subordinates do not always pick up on sarcasm or humor.

4) Don't underestimate communication and its importance to your role as supervisor.

Do

1) Develop your talent to speak clearly, listen actively, and ask questions. Your effectiveness as a supervisor will improve exponentially.

2) Make and maintain eye contact when communicating with another person. It shows you are interested.

3) Make the improvement of communication skills a high priority in your own supervisory development.

VI

Lighting A Fire

Understanding The Concept Of Motivation

An individual's level of motivation is not the panacea for success. For example, I would love to become a professional golfer. I want in the worst way to be another Greg Norman. I am deeply motivated to become a pro. I have hit balls on the driving range until my hands cramp. I would give anything to win the Masters, the U.S. Open, or to be on the Ryder Cup team. But one thing stands in the way—talent or a lack thereof. I am a hacker, and I have always been one. I rarely break 100 on the golf course, even on a good day. No matter how much I am motivated to become a professional golfer, I am never going to realize that dream. So, motivation isn't everything, but it can certainly help the supervisor answer this very important question: Why do people do what they do?

Motivation is a need or desire that influences a person to act. Some would argue that the boss cannot motivate employees, that they must motivate themselves. In some respects this may be true. However, you, as a supervisor, can certainly create a climate in which motivation is possible. As with communication, motivation has been studied on a number of complex levels. But at this point, memorizing some simple motivational rules would be beneficial as you begin your work as a supervisor.

Motivational Rule **1**

The need which is most critical is the need the individual wants satisfied.

Throughout my years as a trainer, I've used a number of successful teaching techniques. One of them is never to tackle any important classroom subject within thirty minutes of the lunch break. The reason quite simply is Rule #1. As the clock ticks toward lunch, students cease to concentrate on learning. The more critical need they want satisfied, their physical appetite, supersedes their desire to learn.

As you get comfortable with your employees, you will become accustomed to their individual levels of performance. So if their performance suddenly drops, you can almost always assume that some critical need has surfaced which is interfering with their attention to their job. Whether it is a physical need such as fatigue or illness, or a more complex issue such as security or self-esteem, it becomes your problem as supervisor if it impacts job performance and persists beyond a short time frame.

It is prudent to avoid a knee-jerk response when these symptoms first come to your attention. On the other hand, you have a responsibility to the organization to intervene if employee performance continues to suffer. Should this be the case, it will be necessary for you to address the problem.

I once had a good employee who uncharacteristically began coming in late for work almost on a daily basis. She was frequently late enough that co-workers began to notice and grumble. Through informal discussions, I made several unsuccessful attempts to identify her problem. Only when I was forced to take disciplinary action did she share with me that her husband had lost his job, and that she was sitting up half the night, every night, worrying about how the bills were going to get paid. When morning arrived, she couldn't get herself out of bed in time to get to work. To make a long story short, the organization helped them find a financial counselor who assisted them with their difficulty. In a short period of time, my employee was back on track. Obviously, not all employee problems are this simple, but regardless of the complexity, you can't help your employees until you know the critical need they want satisfied. Once identified, the solution, although not necessarily simple, will hopefully be straightforward. Whenever an employee problem develops, look first to motivational Rule #1. It may well shortcut the road to the solution.

Motivational Rule **2**

Once a need is satisfied, it is no longer a motivator.

Abraham Maslow created a needs hierarchy to explain the concept of motivation. He hypothesized that once an individual satisfied one type of need, he/she then moved on to satisfy other needs because the need already satisfied was no longer a motivator. In other words, the critical need, once satisfied, no longer is the critical need. As an instructor, I would have little success rewarding my students with food after they come back from lunch. Their hunger is already satisfied; hence, it is no longer a motivator. The application for the supervisor is, of course, to figure out a way to keep the carrot in front of the donkey. Good supervision is more than knowing the rules. It is knowing how to work within those rules to keep the employee motivated, ever marching toward the achievement of organizational goals. It is a tricky little piece of business, but vital to overall productivity.

Motivational Rule 3

The need levels of an individual will change due to changes in the individual or changes in the environment.

This rule is most clearly exemplified by the fact that boys eventually lose interest in frogs. As we said before, people and organizations are both dynamic. They change-and as they change, their need levels change also. At this point, it is important to reemphasize your need to stay in touch with your subordinates. As they mature in the organization, their motivational needs will also diversify. Your loyalty to your employees will, in part, be measured by your success at staying one step ahead of what it takes to keep them happy and productive.

What Did He Just Say?

Don't

1) Don't expect motivation to be the only ingredient necessary for success. In some instances, motivation alone is simply not enough.
2) Don't knee jerk every time an employee's performance fluctuates. He/she may just be having a bad day.
3) Don't abdicate your supervisory responsibility. You must create an environment where motivation can occur.

Do

1) Learn these three motivational rules, and commit them to memory.

2) Ask yourself frequently, "Why is this employee doing things in this manner?" It will help you identify the needs the employee wants satisfied.

3) If a performance problem persists, do not hesitate to get involved. It is your supervisory responsibility to get to the heart of the problem.

4) Always look for new, creative, motivational techniques. As the employee's need levels change, so must your response.

VII

A Pat On The Back
Showing Appreciation For Positive Performance

As a new supervisor, nothing will please you more than a subordinate who consistently performs well. Unfortunately, today's supervisor is so mired down with day-to-day problems that good performance regularly gets ignored rather than praised. The reason this happens is due to a very common supervisory mind-set. Most supervisors see their job as one of identifying and fixing problems. So, if a supervisor has a subordinate who does his/her job, does it well, never complains, and seldom requires guidance, the supervisor inadvertently ignores that employee—"If it ain't broke, don't fix it."

Get out of that state of mind! There may be no need to fix it, but there most certainly is a need to nurture it.

Great employees are not a dime a dozen. In fact, if you get a handful in your entire supervisory career you can consider yourself lucky. Identifying and recognizing good performance should be a high priority with you. Employees need to be told that they are doing well.It keeps them energetic, motivated, and loyal to the organization. Oh, and one more thing; it makes you look good as the boss.

It isn't difficult to do. The words, "Please," "Thank you," and "I appreciate the good job you do," work wonders. Stop and think about it. When was the last time your supervisor complimented you for the good job you do? If it has been anytime recently, then you are indeed fortunate. It is absolutely amazing how many subordinates say, "My boss climbs all over me when I do something wrong, but he doesn't even bother to say 'thanks' for all the good things I do." There's only so much internal satisfaction that employees can muster. If they are not reminded regularly that they are appreciated, they will eventually begin to assume the opposite.

And here's another very important point. When you do go out of your way to express gratitude to your subordinate, don't expect him/her to openly acknowledge your compliment. No one wants to be branded as the boss's special boy or girl. Just accept that they appreciate it, even if they don't show it.

Several years ago, I had a very special employee. He did a fine job and made me look good in the process. One day, after a particularly good piece of work on his part, I penned him a short thank-you memorandum and placed it into his mailbox. I happened to be standing in the corner of the mailroom the next day when he pulled the memo out. He read the note and then commented to his partner, "Well, if I had this note and a quarter, I might be able to buy a cup of coffee." Then he wadded the memo up, threw it on the floor, and walked away. I was livid. The thought that I had gone to the trouble to compliment him and had been openly disparaged in return was unconscionable to me. My first response was to never recognize him again, regardless of how well he performed. But after a few minutes, I calmed down and tried to reason through what had happened. I realized then that what my subordinate had done was simply put on a show for a co-worker. He probably did appreciate the note, but he wasn't going to exhibit that feeling in front of a peer who might then spread the word that the supervisor had a "favorite son." The story has an interesting ending. I retrieved the wrinkled note from the mailroom floor and placed it into my desk. Then I began to watch very closely for another chance to compliment this same employee. It didn't take long because he was such a great worker. As soon as I saw him do something else well, I pulled the note out, unwrinkled it, changed the date, scribbled a new message on it, taped a quarter to it so he could buy a cup of coffee, and placed it back into his mailbox. The next day, he showed up in my office, note in hand, with a sheepish look on his face. Needless to say, he really did appreciate the recognition; and I learned an important lesson about the need to say "thank you" with no strings attached.

Most of you at the supervisory level will not have access to any tangible means of organizational reward. Cash bonuses, raises, transfers, and promotions are usually relegated to the control of upper management. So you must become resourceful, and maybe even willing to spend a little of your own money, to show your subordinates how grateful you are for their good work. Public praise, thank-you notes, special plaques or certificates, buying lunch, or even bringing in doughnuts are relatively inexpensive endeavors, but clearly demonstrate gratitude to your employees.

Remember how you as a supervisor are going to be evaluated. It will be based upon how well you get others to do their job. Your employees love to be appreciated. And in the long term, your show of appreciation to them will work in your supervisory best interests.

What Did He Just Say?

Don't

1) Don't ignore a good employee just because he/she is not a problem. Encourage and praise good job performance.

2) Don't expect any kind of open response when you compliment an employee. Most don't want others to think they are the supervisor's pet.

3) Don't say thank-you one time and assume that's enough. Employees must be praised regularly.

Do

1) Praise your subordinates publicly. Let others know that you recognize and appreciate individual good performance.

2) Look just as hard for good performance as you do for behavior that needs to be corrected.

3) Become creative in how you express your gratitude. A small investment will generate huge returns.

VIII

A Slap On The Wrist
Handling Inappropriate Employee Behavior

Addressing inappropriate behavior is always a troublesome responsibility for supervisors. People do not like being told that they have done something wrong. Some human relations specialists even argue that there is no such thing as constructive criticism. Regardless, your employees are human beings. They will make mistakes both in procedure and judgment. If you are to score high on your supervisory report card, you must be prepared to handle admonition, correction, and discipline in a prompt, professional manner.

Seldom will discipline emerge as your first course of action. Absent some sort of criminal violation, or heinous breach of organization policy, most first offenses can be handled with supervisory coaching and counseling. It is imperative, however, to document these activities because questions may arise down the road at grievance hearings, arbitrations, or even in litigation.

An effective supervisor does not continually threaten yet never follow through. Your employees need to know from the start that you mean business. As distasteful as it might be, you must use the disciplinary process decisively when it becomes necessary. You must also be well versed in the limits of your disciplining authority. Most organizations relegate certain discipline authorization to certain levels of company management. You would certainly not want to threaten a demotion or transfer if it were not within your purview to impose such discipline.

It is always important to remember that your job as a supervisor is to criticize poor performance without personally attacking the performer. You are acting as a professional organizational representative, not as an individual who has been personally harmed by the employee's inappropriate actions. However, understand that the natural reaction from subordinates is usually anger directed at you because you are, in fact, the one who is delivering the bad news. For that reason, your method of delivery becomes significant. It is every bit as important that you discipline in private as it is that you praise in public. Employees react with unpredictable emotions when receiving discipline. No one likes it, but some take it very hard. Reaction may run the gambit from anger, to guilt, to a complete emotional breakdown. Regardless, you should be empathic, and provide them an environment where they can react and recover away from others. Should the instance arise where the employee is simply too emotional to return to work, you as a supervisor may even need to assist him/her in privately leaving the building, or even by driving him/her home.

Consistency must be your permanent companion when dealing with employee discipline. Discipline review and grievance adjustment boards make every attempt to compare disciplines across the board to ensure consistent application. Any punishment you mete out that appears to deviate from past discipline for similar violations will almost always be reversed. More importantly, the message your subordinates should get from watching you is that although they may not like the discipline you impose, they know they are getting as fair a shake as someone else under your supervision who committed a similar infraction.

Earlier in this book you were cautioned to walk softly and be prudent with the use of your newly awarded power. Relative to the appropriate use of discipline, however, your new subordinates will wonder whether or not you have the intestinal fortitude to slap their wrist when necessary. If you are reluctant or indecisive when it comes to disciplining inappropriate behavior, your employees will be quick to sense it. Believe it or not, subordinates derive a great deal of comfort from knowing that their supervisor is in control, and will not tolerate poor performance or bad behavior.

As a final note, it should be said that after all is said and done, there is still a job to do. You are still the supervisor; he/she is still your subordinate; and you must assist the offended employee in getting back down to business. I have seen situations where feelings became so hardened that supervisors and employees refused to talk to one another for months after a disciplinary event. This is unacceptable. If you sense this attitude on the part of a recently disciplined subordinate, confront the problem directly. At least let the injured employee know that you still value his/her contribution to the organization and that the inappropriate action did not impact your opinion of him/her as a person. It will not change things overnight, but you can take comfort in the fact that you have done everything within your power to ameliorate the situation.

What Did He Just Say?

Don't

1) In most instances, don't look to discipline as your first step in corrective action. Find out why the inappropriate behavior occurred and respond accordingly.

2) When it comes time to discipline an employee, don't hesitate. Confirm that your action is proper, then take it.

3) Don't impose discipline by the seat of your pants. Do the research necessary to confirm what has been done in the past for similar violations.

Do

1) Be professional but empathetic during the imposition of discipline. All subordinates react differently, some very emotionally.

2) Make sure to coach, criticize, and discipline in private. Give the employee time to recover before returning to work.

3) Be professional and courteous. Ensure that the subordinate knows that the discipline is not personal.

4) Once discipline has been completed, help the employee get back on track as quickly as possible.

IX

A Flip Of The Coin
Making Good Decisions

One of the best illustrations of indecisiveness I ever witnessed was during a supervisor's conference where a group of us were venting about our individual supervisory problems. Describing a situation with his work group, one of the attendees made the comment, "I'm so frustrated with my peoples' indecisiveness. I just don't know what I'm going to do." Duh! Whose example do you think his subordinates might be following?

The fact that you have been promoted is a pretty good sign that you are not afraid to make decisions. That's good, because one thing subordinates cannot stand is a supervisor who is indecisive. When you are in a position to determine issues which affect them daily, and you are either unwilling or unable to do so, your credibility is diminished, and your lack of leadership shows.

But there's more to it than that. Obviously, the precursor to making good decisions is to be decisive. Custer made a decision at Bull Run. Napoleon made a decision at Waterloo. Nixon made a decision during Watergate. History has taught us that none of these decisions were considered to be particularly good.

So how do you go about making good decisions? As with everything in supervision, there is no precise formula. And clearly, decision–making ranges from the very simple algorithmic decisions to complex problem-solving. But there are some basic tenets which, when followed, seem to direct you toward better decisions.

Initially, you should avoid making any decision in a vacuum. It is called linear thinking, and it is a very shallow thought process. It assumes each problem has a single solution, and it views every decision as discrete, singular, and unique. It supposes that the decision will remain valid forever, with no effect on any other part of the organization. This is the type of thinking you see in a day care center. Small children who are still learning about cause and effect see their world as one where, "If I do this, then something happens which is good for me." They do not consider the long-range implications of their decisions. In the workplace, decision-making of this type ignores the interrelationships among organizational elements, and may, in the long run, contribute to a larger problem. Linear thinking places too much emphasis on the speed with which the decision is made, and too little emphasis on information gathering. The trick here is to balance both without over emphasizing one or the other. Seeking too much information, or getting too many people involved in the research process can result in analysis paralysis where nothing ever gets accomplished. Some of the best ideas around have been destroyed by sending them to a committee for decision. What's more, 100% of the information needed to make a decision is of no value if it arrives two days late. If you have a majority of the information necessary to make the decision, make it and move on.

Systems thinking, on the other hand, is a much better decision-making vehicle. Systems thinking assumes the opposite of linear thinking. It realizes that decisions are interrelated and may impact other organizational entities. It also views decision-making as a dynamic process where problems are not isolated and decisions may only be good for a certain period of time. Supervisors who use a systems thinking approach are thinking globally. They are reaching beyond the immediate short-term resolution to examine the long-range ramifications of their decision.

Now clearly, routine day-to-day decisions will not require a sophisticated approach like systems thinking. However, the supervisor who makes a habit of using a systems approach whenever possible will make better, more well-rounded decisions all the time.

On occasion, you will find yourself in the position where making a certain decision has both positive and negative ramifications. That does not preclude you from making the decision, but it does require that you ask an additional question, which is, "What is best for the organization?" If your decision is favorable for both your employee and the organization, then there is no problem. If, however, a decision has a contrary impact on one or the other, you must always decide in favor of the organization. Not only is it your responsibility, but it prevents impulsive decision-making which you will never be able to justify to your subordinates.

Finally, not every decision you make is going to have a predictable, or even a desirable outcome. None of us has a crystal ball, and only hindsight is 20/20. For that reason, you always weigh the value of your decision at the time you make the decision, not after you see the outcome. Suppose you decide to take a drive along a certain road. While in route you are rear-ended by another driver. That doesn't mean your decision was bad, even though the outcome was negative. On the other hand, deciding to drive home while you are under the influence of alcohol is a bad decision, even if the outcome is that you arrive safely. We all learn from our experience, and provided it is not peppered with too many failures, we profit from it and become better. Making good decisions is not luck. It is a skill which is developed through conscious effort and persistence. If you follow all the right steps, and the decision turns out badly, don't be discouraged. Keep trying and keep learning. The greatest barrier to success is not in doing wrong; it is in doing nothing.

What Did He Just Say?

Don't

1) Don't pass up the opportunity to appear decisive. It gives your subordinates confidence in your supervisory ability.
2) Don't be a linear thinker. It is a short-term way of thinking which is not effective.
3) Don't study something to death before acting. Gather as much information as possible, then act.

Do

1) Use a systems thinking approach to make your decisions. It results in a more global decision which is better for the organization.
2) When faced with a decision which has both a positive and negative impact, always make your decision based upon what is best for the organization.
3) Weigh the value of your decision at the time you make the decision, not when you see the outcome.

X

What Part Of "NO" Don't You Understand?
Handling Employee Requests

Handling employee requests should be pretty straightforward, right? Isn't the answer either "yes" or "no"? Unfortunately, it's not quite that simple. Sometimes the answer can be "maybe." Other times the answer is "no," although it used to be "yes." Sometimes it is "yes" for one employee and "no" for another. And when the answer is not what your subordinate wants to hear, some type of explanation is generally anticipated.

Make no mistake. Your subordinates compare notes. If you handle one employee's request one way, and another's in a different way, you will be forced to explain why and may find yourself in a predicament from which escape is very difficult.

I have always tried to accommodate the requests of my subordinates whenever possible, provided the request was legitimate and did not conflict with the overall mission. Creating rules to control such accommodation is generally a good idea, providing you apply them consistently across the board.

I once had a rule that only two of my nine subordinates could be off on any given day. It was commonly known throughout the office and had worked well during my relatively short tenure as their supervisor. One afternoon, a subordinate enthusiastically entered my office with news that he had won an all expenses paid three-day offshore fishing trip for him and his wife the next weekend. In order to go on the trip, he needed the next Monday off. I checked the schedule and discovered that two other subordinates were already scheduled off for that day. Once informed, he scurried off to see if he could trade vacation days with one of them. When that didn't work, he hustled back to see me. I felt sorry for him, but I reiterated my rule, and denied his request. He just sat and looked at me. I eventually broke the silence by explaining why I had the rule in the first place. He continued to just look at me. It was beginning to get somewhat uncomfortable, so I explained further that if three people were off at the same time, others had to assume too much of the group's workload. He just stared. Before long I was feeling an immense amount of pressure from his silent assertiveness. After what seemed like an interminable period of silence, he looked at me and quietly murmured, "Boss, please?"

I succumbed. He jumped up, shook my hand, and raced out of my office. The satisfaction that I felt at having terminated an uncomfortable interaction was short-lived when I realized what I had done. This subordinate had come to me with a special request to be sure. But what was to happen the next time an employee wanted time off, and it violated the rule? By stepping outside the lines to accommodate one employee, I had weakened my integrity with those who would have to carry the extra workload and with everyone who had played by the rules up to that point.

The next week, I called for a mandatory meeting. When all nine subordinates, as well as my own boss had assembled, I walk to the front of the room, faced them and said this:

> *Ladies and gentlemen, last week I made a mistake. I violated my own rule and let three people off on one day. The reason I did it was because I felt pressured to accommodate a special request. I was wrong. I now realize that in so doing, I unfairly tasked those of you who were working to carry an unrealistic burden. I apologize to each of you for my error. It will not happen again.*

Everyone left the meeting with a clear understanding of how and why I had violated my rule and what the practice would be in the future. But look at the humiliating process I had to go through to repair the damage I had caused. Take my word for it...the first time you compromise your parameters, you begin to lose control. Before long, your attempts to please everybody become arbitrary, impulsive, and unfair. And to stand before your subordinates admitting mistakes and asking for forgiveness is difficult, humbling, and will only work once or twice.

By the same token, this is not to say that you as the supervisor should never allow your subordinates to try out new ideas, or to be creative on the job. If an employee requests to handle a particular job task in a unique manner, and he/she makes a good argument for doing so, it can be in everyone's best interests to grant the request. Whether the idea works or not, it encourages your employees to get imaginative and to think outside the box.

Granting requests is always popular, and it promotes a comfortable working environment for both you and your subordinates. But it is your duty as a supervisor to remain cognizant of the broader implications that accompany every "yes" or "no" answer. Things like job performance, advance notice, emergencies, use and abuse of sick time, potential work conflicts, and established rules and policies must be considered when deciding how to handle the requests of your subordinates. You will certainly want to provide them with as many job benefits as you can reasonably allow. But, you are not competing in a popularity contest. Sometimes the answer has to be the one the employee doesn't want to hear. Like it or not, it's part of the charge you accepted when you became a supervisor.

What Did He Just Say?

Don't

1) Don't try to handle employee requests in an arbitrary, impulsive manner. You'll be in deep trouble before you know it.

2) Don't violate your own rules for handling requests unless you can articulate an acceptable reason for doing so.

3) Don't measure your success by how popular you are. Concentrate on doing the right things in the right way.

Do

1) Always consider the larger and long-term consequences before deciding how to handle an employee request.

2) If you handle a request inappropriately, admit it, fix it, and try not to repeat the error.

3) If an employee requests to try something unique and innovative, consider the risk involved, and if possible allow him/her to try it.

XI

Sit! Speak! Rollover!
Training Your Employees

The majority of your subordinates will do what is expected of them on the job. They will even do it your way, provided you insure that they know how. Training is one of your primary responsibilities as a supervisor. And frankly, the legacy you leave will be played out through your subordinates. Given that, you must realize the importance of training, and evidence it through your supervisory style. The unfortunate truth is that training is the red-headed stepchild of most organizations. They may maintain some type of a training section, but seldom want to sacrifice employee service time to fulfill in-service training needs. I've found it this way throughout my experience, and, with the exception of the most creative, innovative companies, the trend will likely continue.

So, you can accept that prediction and do nothing for your employees, or you can become proactive and create training opportunities for them. This will reward you with an immediate increase in employee productivity as well as the long-term satisfaction of knowing that you helped enhance their careers.

One of the greatest teaching techniques you can use with your employees is accomplished without cracking the first textbook. It's called modeling the behavior you expect from them. Now, I'm not talking so much about the actual job skills as I'm talking about attitude and professionalism. A high percentage of what human beings learn is by watching. So if you believe something well enough to preach it, but not well enough to practice it, your employees are going to get confused and frustrated.

I once had a supervisor who played golf every Friday afternoon. When he was finished, he scurried back to the office to make sure all of us subordinates had kept our noses to the grindstone until the formal close of business. Confusing and frustrating!

Similarly, our work group received a memorandum from another supervisor that read in part:

> ...Many of you are rushing through your paperwork without proofreading it properly. For that reason, employees who continue to submit improperly written reports will be marked down on **there** (sic) upcoming evaluations.

Confusing and frustrating!

On another occasion, my hot-tempered supervisor was late to a work function I had scheduled because of a traffic jam that occurred on a major roadway. Later, during an angry diatribe directed at me, he screamed, "...You were the one who picked the place; you were the one who set the time; you were in charge of scheduling, and it is your job to PREDICT when and where the traffic jams will occur." Yeah, sure. Me and my crystal ball. Confusing and frustrating!

Unfortunately, much of the behavior we observe by watching our supervisory models is bad. But you can make a conscious decision not to be that way. Show your employees that you put enough credence in your talk to live it out in the details of your supervisory life. It will speak volumes about both your supervisory and leadership style.

Relative to teaching the job function itself, I have discovered that neither "telling" nor "demonstrating" is very effective without allowing the employee to practice and/or simulate the desired new behavior. For example, telling someone how to play chords on a guitar would be an extremely ineffective method of teaching the guitar. Even watching a trained player demonstrate how to go from chord to chord would result in frustration, if the model moved too quickly or showed too many changes at one time. With that in mind, I have learned to use a three-step process to train and encourage new behaviors. First, use an appropriate trainer to teach the behavior (Hire a guitar instructor). This person should be someone who not only knows what you want, but knows how to teach others to do it. Remember, when I speak of your responsibility to train, I don't mean you actually have to do the training. Just because you're the supervisor, doesn't make you the subject matter expert in everything (although some supervisors think it does). By simply facilitating the training, you are accomplishing your mission. Secondly, allow the employee to practice the behavior under simulated work conditions (Provide them a guitar). This may be a bit risky, but it instills tremendous employee self-confidence, and puts the training to work right away. Finally, give the employee written manuals, verbal encouragement, and advanced training as necessary to support the learning and job performance after the initial training (Give them guitar music books).

You will have to get creative if you plan to make ongoing training a part of your employee development plan. Obviously, you can't send everyone away at one time. You may not even be able to employ conventional classroom education methodology. But with all of the different training approaches available, you will not only be successful at identifying new training techniques, you will have a great deal of fun in the process. For years, I employed a training method where I allowed a subordinate to select a job-related subject, research the subject at will, then present his/her findings in two consecutive fifteen-minute employee training sessions. With only twelve people in the group, we maintained this training regimen for over two years. No one was overworked, and we all learned.

There's an old German proverb that says, "Ve grow too soon oldt, und too late schmart." Such could be said for most employees inside the organization. But by helping your employees grow "schmarter" sooner, you will benefit in ways you cannot yet see. A famous educator once said that the most valuable result of education is the ability to do the thing you have to do, when it ought to be done, whether you like it or not. If you can teach that to your subordinates, you have imparted both wisdom and discipline.

What Did He Just Say?

Don't

1) Don't rely on the organization to train your employees. Get creative and help them yourself.

2) Don't expect your subordinates to put stock in things you say unless you reinforce them through your actions.

3) Don't just tell your employees what you want. Train them, let them practice on the job, and reinforce their learning.

Do

1) Look for new, innovative ways to introduce in-service training to your subordinates. Videos, books, games, and guest presentations are all effective.

2) Consider subordinate development and training to be one of your most important responsibilities as a supervisor.

3) Be patient with subordinates while they learn. A valuable return sometimes requires a vigorous investment up front.

XII

Gee, Boss, It Wasn't Me!
Why Employees Lie

If you think your subordinates are always going to tell you the truth, you are very naïve. It might sound like I'm talking out of both sides of my mouth when I tell you on one hand to "trust your employees," then say on the other that they are going to lie to you. Actually, I am not.

They won't lie all the time, about everything. And the things they misrepresent to you won't always impact important or sensitive issues. They won't all be great big lies. They might just be variations on the truth, or just a part of the entire story, or maybe mostly factual information with a spin on it that changes the context.

Employees are always out to protect themselves in the work arena. Even as children, they learned that lying works, at least some of the time. And for the most part, they don't mean anything personal toward you. They do it for a number of reasons, and you, as a new supervisor, should be aware of at least some of them.

I once had an excellent employee who worked for me in a very sensitive document procurement and distribution area of the organization. One day, I tasked him with the responsibility of retrieving and delivering a very important set of organizational papers to our legal section. When the legal section called the next week screaming frantically that they had never gotten the plans, I immediately queried my employee. He insisted that he had personally delivered the missing documents the previous Saturday. He even explained exactly where he had placed the papers. I told him to meet with the legal people and explain what he did. He returned stating that the papers were not where he had left them, and he had no idea where they were. Frankly, this was a serious situation, because the plans were very confidential, and could be harmful if they fell into the wrong hands. During two additional interviews, my employee remained adamant that he had delivered the papers appropriately. I was completely baffled. Because we worked in such a sensitive area, we were subject to periodic polygraph examinations. I had no other choice. Something was certainly wrong here, but I wanted to absolve my employee of the blame. He agreed to take a polygraph exam and arrived at the appointed time. Although I was not present, the polygrapher later shared with me the conversation he had with my employee. When the employee arrived, the polygrapher said to him, "In a minute, we will begin the formal test. But before we do, I want to ask you one more time. Did you deliver the papers to the legal section as instructed?" My employee thought for a moment and responded, "Well, no I guess I didn't." When asked why he hadn't just been honest up front, he replied, "I misplaced the papers, then forgot about them. I just didn't want my boss to be disappointed in me."

As convoluted as it sounds, employees will sometimes think that way. They will make an honest error, then risk losing their job in an effort to cover it up. My employee was terminated just because he didn't want me to be disappointed in him. Didn't he think I'd be disappointed when I found out he had lied to me three or four times? Silly as it sounds, it happens.

A second reason employees lie is that they know it ensures success. Remember the employee who won the fishing trip and needed the Monday off? He played a dangerous game when he came to me suggesting that it would be O.K. for me to violate one of my own supervisory rules. It worked because of my supervisory weakness, but it was much riskier than just calling in sick. Because he was an employee who never abused his sick time, I would never have suspected that he would feign an illness just to go fishing. He probably did give some serious thought to calling in sick, but opted out because he had already told too many people about the trip. It would have increased his chances of getting caught. But you can take this to the bank. If lying ensures a success which cannot otherwise be achieved, and the issue is important enough to the employee, he/she will weigh the risk, and more times than not, take the chance.

Some employees don't tell you the truth because they don't really believe you want to hear the truth. Even your best employees can be guilty of this...and it's probably your fault. I had a boss once who made a big deal out of calling us into his office and spouting off about a new idea or plan he had created. Then he would ask our opinion. The minute someone said something contradictory to what he wanted to hear, he would shake his head back and forth, interrupt the talker in mid-sentence, and say something like, "I guess you didn't hear me right. Let me see if I can put it in simpler terms that you can understand. Pay attention this time."

I have to admit that he made me so angry with his "holier-than–thou, know-it-all pomposity," that I personally vowed NEVER to help him by offering my true opinion. Why should I bother? He didn't want it anyway. All he wanted was support for what he'd already decided. If employees are not convinced that you are really interested in what they think, they'll just tell you what they believe you want to hear, then go on about their business. If this happens, you have all but isolated yourself from people who could really help you.

Finally, employees will lie as a means of spontaneous defense. Several years ago, I walked into the kitchen and caught my five-year-old daughter with her hand in the cookie jar.

I asked, "Hey, what are you doing?"

"Nothing," she replied.

I said, "It looks like to me you're trying to get a cookie."

"But, I'm not," she affirmed.

She had literally been caught with her hand in the cookie jar. Even so, her insinuated defense was, "Are you going to believe me or your lying eyes?"

Employees are much like children in this respect. If you catch them in an awkward situation and corner them with it, they'll strike back with the first thing that comes to mind. It is usually some sort of denial. In other words, you can compel them to lie because of the timing and method you used to ask the question. Good supervisors look for alternate methods which get at the truth without accusation.

One day, a company driver under my supervision called a pedestrian a jackass because the pedestrian jaywalked in front of his truck. The pedestrian happened to be the president of a prominent bank in town. He obtained the number on the truck and complained to me about the driver's behavior. We were a very image-conscious company, and I knew I would have to confront the driver. I also knew that if I caught him off-guard by questioning him in an accusatory tone, he might feel forced to lie about it. Instead, I called him into the office and this is what I said:

> Bob, I don't want you to say a word yet. I just want you to listen
> to me. In a minute I'm going to ask you a question. The question
> is, 'Did you call a pedestrian a jackass today?' If your answer is

'yes,' I'll reprimand you for it, and it will be over. If you lie about it, I can guarantee it will go much harder for you. Now, did you call a pedestrian a jackass today? He got this impish grin on his face and answered, 'Yeah, I called him that; but he had it coming!' Then he proceeded to tell his side of the story.

By going about it in that way, it made both of us winners. I got a confession to a minor indiscretion, without making Bob feel compelled to lie as a means of spontaneous defense. It never hurts to slow the situation down, allow some of the emotion to dissipate, and think of just how to word the questions before engaging an employee in a sensitive conversation.

Lying is a survival mechanism. It's not always innocent, to be sure. Sometimes, it can be political, vicious, and severe. But you cannot eliminate it. You must learn to work around it. You do so by asking the right questions, in the right way; then by listening to what your employees say, to what they don't say, and to what they would like to say, but can't. It is a specialized form of communication that takes skill and practice. The better you get at it, the better supervisor you'll be.

What Did He Just Say?

Don't

1) Don't be naïve. Every employee has the potential to lie to you.
2) Don't ask an employee's opinion unless you really want it. To do so compromises his/her honesty and your supervisory integrity.
3) Don't force your employees to lie by asking rapid-fire, emotional questions.

Do

1) Learn how to listen and filter information from your subordinates. It will help you determine the whole truth.
2) Realize that, although it can't be condoned, employees will lie as a means of organization survival. They seldom intend anything harmful or personal toward you as the supervisor.
3) Clearly explain your philosophy about employee honesty from the very beginning. You may save yourself a problem later.

XIII

There's Got To Be A Better Way
Encouraging Employee Creativity

A philosophy professor announced to his class that their final examination would be in the form of an essay. On the appointed day, the professor placed a chair in front of the room. He told his students that they had two hours to write an essay proving that the chair existed. As the students began to ponder and labor over the task before them, one student sat straight up, put pencil to paper and wrote, "What chair?" He then submitted his paper and left.

Was it what the professor expected? Probably not. But you must admit it was creative, and it challenged the traditional way of looking at a problem.

Organizations are slow to change. The bigger the organization, the more valid this seems. But it can still be fun to try the same old things in new ways, and sometimes the new way proves to be very effective.

One year, I supervised a group of process servers. Our productivity was measured by the number of subpoenas we could place into the hands of the right people. One particular service problem was a young man by the name of Thomas Banks. Two previous attempts had been made to his address with no success. Both servers said, "A guy answers the door and is friendly enough, but he says Banks doesn't live there anymore." At the end of a particular workday, I called all six servers together and said, "We only have one more shot at this guy. Someone get creative and come back tomorrow with an idea that will work." The next morning one of my servers asked me for the subpoena. She came back an hour later and announced that the subpoena had been successfully served. When we asked her secret, she said, "It was easy. I just went to the door and knocked. When the guy answered, I said,

'I have a subpoena for Nicolas Brown. Is he here?'

The guy replied, 'No one by that name lives here.'

I said, 'O.K. What's your name?'

He answered, 'Thomas Banks.'

I then placed the paper into his hand and said, 'Consider yourself served.'"

Creativity does not have to be rocket science. It is simply a matter of stepping outside the traditional arena and looking at something from a different perspective. As a supervisor, you may experience difficulty infusing this concept into the routine of your subordinates. As with everything else, it helps if you first set the example. The following story illustrates my point.

After numerous attempts to get my subordinates to become more creative, one of my employees named Marilyn finally approached me with the idea of rotating the assistant supervisor position among all the subordinates so that everyone could get a little taste of supervisory responsibility. Frankly, I was cool to the concept; but since it was the only creative suggestion anyone had proffered, I decided to use it as an example. I went to my boss and told him my plan.

Long story short, the idea was a complete disaster. My full-time assistant was miffed at having to give up his position, newer employees felt uncomfortable during their tenure, other employees let the job go to their head and didn't want to give it up, and everyone was frustrated by the instability it caused. It took approximately two months to complete the rotation. When it was over, I restored my full-time assistant to the position and called for an employee meeting. After I had completed all the routine business, I thanked everyone for their cooperation during the experiment and called Marilyn to the front of the room. My boss then presented her with a beautifully framed certificate, signed by the executive manager, naming her creative employee of the quarter. You could have heard a pin drop; then the applause erupted. Later, my assistant asked me why I would present an award for an idea that had turned out to be so terrible. My response to him was that new ideas should be treated as though they were baby fish. In stocking a lake or stream, thousands of baby fish are placed in the water. Only a few survive, but those few are enough. Oh, by the way, the next week I received five new ideas from five different subordinates. It's always amazing what a little recognition can do.

Of course, it is always possible that you will have no success at encouraging creativity among your employees, regardless of how hard you try. In those instances, you yourself must become the creative spark, then translate your plans into specific tasks which your subordinates can accomplish.

During one of my many years in law enforcement, I supervised a group of nine veteran patrol officers. Each of these street cops had been on the force for at least ten years. They showed up every day and did their job, but not with a great deal of enthusiasm. One day at line-up, I ask them to help me come up with a creative idea to address the high number of traffic crashes we were experiencing in our sector. No one had any suggestions. As a matter of fact, over the next week, I spoke with each officer personally, but to no avail. I finally realized that "If it was to be, it was up to me."

From a computer readout, I identified the nine highest traffic accident intersections in the sector. At our next line-up, I presented my idea. Each officer would be assigned an intersection. During their uncommitted time, they were to monitor their intersection for traffic violations. Each officer was instructed to document at least nine traffic contacts per eight-hour tour of duty. It did not matter whether they gave warnings, wrote citations, or made arrests, as long as they made formal contact with nine or more violators. Everyone understood the assignment. No one had questions. At the end of the day, I tallied the total number of traffic contacts the squad had conducted. I was not surprised to find exactly 81 contacts. Each officer had done the very minimum—no more, no less. Had they embraced my idea enthusiastically? Hardly. But they had followed my lead, and perhaps they did more than they would have done had I not come up with a plan.

Creativity is an intangible. It is difficult to measure and evaluate. Some people are naturally creative, while others cling to traditional methods for stability and reassurance. Good supervisors try to strike a balance. There is always a better way to do something. Be on the lookout for it. Encourage your subordinates to try new ideas, and support them, even if the idea fails. In fact, most of them will. But if, in the process, you stumble on something that makes the organization better, you have made a valuable contribution.

What Did He Just Say?

Don't

1) Don't be satisfied with the same old way of doing things. Encourage your employees to grow creatively.
2) Don't be discouraged when ideas fail. Most of them do. Quickly move on and try something else.
3) Don't expect all of your subordinates to be creative. It may be that the responsibility for creativity will fall to you, the supervisor.

Do

1) Look for creative ways to keep the same old job fun and productive.
2) Recognize and reward subordinates who come up with new and refreshing ways to get the work accomplished. It will inspire additional creativity.
3) If your employees are not creative types, you must develop the plan; then translate it into measurable, workable things your subordinates can do.

XIV

"Because I Said So"
Dealing With Troublesome Employees

If one hasn't been assigned to you yet, stand by. He or she is on the way. Troublesome employees are the supervisor's cross to bear. In many respects, they are your trial by fire, because if all subordinates were great, everything I'm telling you to do would be fairly easy. Unfortunately, that's not the way things work inside the organization.

Let me say at the outset that every employee who causes you a particular problem is not necessarily a troublesome employee. Employees who are dealing with adversity, new employees who make mistakes while learning their job, employees with whom you do not see eye-to-eye, and even employees who might question your

authority, require time and energy; but they are not, by my defini-
tion, troublesome. Troublesome employees are the ones who come
to work with a chip on their shoulder; do as little as possible to earn
a paycheck; feel that the organization owes them more than they are
receiving; do the wrong things in the wrong ways; and see it, not as
a duty, but as a benefit to make your supervisory life as miserable as
possible. They come in several varieties. Over the years I have cate-
gorized them into five groups: Whiners, Shuckers, Punchinellos,
Scrappers, and Mutts.

Whiners started crying when the doctor spanked their newborn
butt, and they haven't stopped since. They bellyache primarily
because it gets them what they want. They had parents who gave
them everything just to shut them up, and they have found that the
same techniques work for them on the job. They whimper, com-
plain, moan, and snivel at every turn; and have done it for so long,
they don't even realize they do it. Now, as I have said, I don't rec-
ommend public criticism of employees, but I sometimes take the
gloves off when it comes to Whiners. You can't stop them. They're
naturals. But you can slow them down. First, ensure that their whining gets them nowhere with you. This is easier than it sounds
because, if they fail at first to get their way, they will turn up the
intensity a notch. Don't let it phase you. Muscle right through it and
hold them to the same standard you hold for everyone else.
Secondly, let your other subordinates know you are on to the
Whiner's game. I used to bring a golf towel to my supervisory meet-
ings. Whenever my Whiner started up, I would throw the towel to
him and tell him not to get tears all over the floor. The first time I
did it, he was shocked and embarrassed; but I could see the satisfaction on the faces of his peers who now realized I wasn't going to
put up with his antics.

Shuckers don't want to do anything. They are relatively nice people, but they are lazy. They waste as much time as possible visiting
with peers, taking breaks, talking on the phone, reading the paper,
camping out in the bathroom, strolling the halls and playing com-

puter games. They take longer to complete assignments than anyone else, and they are difficult to pin down when you ask for the status of their projects. It sometimes seems they work harder at avoiding work than they would if they just did their job. And, they also interfere with the productivity of other workers. The way you deal with these troublemakers is through the application of basic supervisory techniques. Give them their assignments in written form, complete with your deadline expectations. If they miss the deadline, take away a benefit. Be creative. There is always something you can use as leverage. Expect them to scream bloody murder. They will claim, "foul." Let 'um. Tell them in no uncertain terms that they have a job to do, and you expect them to do it. Watch them like a hawk. When you see them wasting time, call their hand. Before long, they'll begin to work a little harder...at least when they know you are looking.

The term "Punchinello" comes from the fat, humpbacked clown in the Italian puppet shows. It has a very appropriate application for certain troublesome employees in the workplace. Punchinellos are extremely arrogant incompetents who think they are much smarter than they are. They strut around and brag to anyone they can corner. Peers run when they see the Punchinello coming. Even the Schucker would rather work than listen to him/her brag. Punchinellos wax poetic about how they know more, have done it better, been at it longer, and been awarded more honors. They simply can't find anyone more worthy of praise and worship than themselves. To be perfectly honest, they are terrible employees. Because they are too self-absorbed to focus on the overall mission, they direct all their energy toward meaningless, petty minutia; and raise the same silly issues over and over, regardless of the subject under discussion. About the only way you as a supervisor can deal with these types of employees is to work around them. They are too high-headed to recognize their shortcomings, even if you point them out. If you give them anything meaningful or critical to do, they will screw it up. Fortunately, most peers see them for what they are and accept them as a booger on the organization's finger which simply can't be shaken off. Avoid giving them critical tasks and try to keep them from bothering the other workers. It's about all you can do.

Scrappers are mean-spirited employees who derive some perverse satisfaction from constantly generating conflict. They are abrasive, discourteous, critical people who attempt to demonstrate their intelligence by debating everything you present to your work group. Don't ever expect them to be team players. It's not their nature. Take caution not to allow them to draw you into an argument. They are better at it than you, and they never give in. Before long, their contentious nature will force the discourse to deteriorate into an emotional finger-pointing, name-calling, shouting match where nobody wins. You don't beat the Scrapper with a knockout. You have to win on points. So instead of arguing, just cut them off at the pass. If that means embarrassing them by telling them to be quiet, or by reminding them who's the boss, so be it. "Because I said so" has been a catch phrase I have used frequently with Scrappers. It is a phrase they understand, and it usually ends the grumbling...for the time being.

Mutts just don't fit. Unfortunately, there is no organizational dog pound in which to place them. They march to the beat of a different drummer. They never seem to be in sync with the other workers, and they do and say things that force you to go along behind them cleaning up their mess. They are not malicious. They just come from a different planet. Many times, they become the laughingstock or the butt of the jokes, and you have to step in and defend them. Of all your troublesome employees, this one can be your most dangerous. He/she is a loose cannon who is highly unpredictable. Other than keeping an eye out for trouble, the best way to handle the Mutt is with admonition and counseling. They will follow your guidance as best they can. Unfortunately, by the time you counsel them, the damage is already done. They try to do the right things. They just seldom do them in the appropriate way. I once supervised a mutt police officer who was dispatched to deliver a death message.

When he arrived at the residence, no one was home. So he penned a note that read, "Dear Mrs. Jones, Your husband was killed earlier tonight." He stuck it to the screen door, and left. The new widow came home, read the note, and fainted dead away, striking her head on the concrete porch. The first I learned of this employee disaster was when I got a call from her livid brother in the emergency room. Mutts don't mess things up on purpose, but they can turn your hair prematurely gray.

Troublesome employees are the athlete's foot of the organization. They are irritating, insalubrious, and impossible to eradicate. They will measure your supervisory metal daily. And, believe it or not, they will make you better. Any supervisor can deal with good employees. With troublesome employees, your motto must be, "that which does not kill me, makes me better."

What Did He Just Say?

Don't

1) Don't immediately label every employee who has a problem as a troublesome employee.

2) Don't ignore the actions of troublesome employees. A measure of your supervisory skill is determined by how you deal with them.

3) Never respond to their antics by giving in to their demands. Learn to counter them effectively.

4) Don't waste all of your time and energy on your troublesome employees. Your good employees need attention also.

Do

1) Learn the supervisory techniques necessary to deal effectively with troublesome employees.

2) Take whatever action is appropriate, even if it means doing so in front of your other subordinates.

3) Accept troublesome employees as simply part of your supervisory responsibility. They will always be a part of the organization.

XV

**You're Really Not That Bad
Evaluating Your Subordinates**

When I was a young practitioner, employees received a written evaluation from their supervisor every six months. Ratings ranged from unacceptable to outstanding in nine different dimensions, with average being a middle rating. I always received high marks. Following a transfer to a new position, I was assigned to an old veteran supervisor. When I received my first evaluation from him, I was dumbfounded. He had rated me "average" in all nine dimensions, without providing any written explanation whatsoever. In comparing notes with my peers (remember there are very few secrets in an office environment), I discovered that every subordinate who worked for him had received exactly the same rating. They also told me that he had always evaluated that way. I did a little policy research and discovered why. Organizational policy dictated that any time a supervisor awarded a score either above or below "average," he/she was required to attach some form of documentation justifying the rating. This nincompoop was so lazy that he was simply taking the easy way out of a task he considered to be a waste of time.

Six months later, one week before the next evaluation, I asked to speak to him in his office. I gingerly offered up several pages of typed notes outlining my accomplishments as they related to the rating factors, over the last six months. I left a place for him to sign his name at the bottom. I carefully suggested to him that the notes might "assist" him in the preparation of my evaluation. Then I thanked him and left. When the evaluations came out, all of my peers received the same average scores in every dimension. I, however, received an outstanding evaluation, to which he had stapled my own typed notes. Ha! More than one way to skin a cat.

By doing his work for him, I had managed to get a better evaluation. But the point here is that it was a totally unacceptable supervisory behavior which caused persistent feelings of frustration for his subordinates.

Evaluating employee performance is a challenging task for supervisors. It is an inexact science which makes it extremely difficult to eliminate the subjectivity, regardless of the quality of the evaluative instrument you use. Another difficulty is that evaluative honesty is, in many cases, compromised as the supervisor looks to take the easy way out. Employees are almost always rated more highly than they deserve, so that the supervisor can minimize discomfort during the evaluative conference. This is a cowardly technique, and it is unfair to the subordinate.

Should you rate your subordinates honestly regardless of the consequences? Absolutely. But there are some things you can do to minimize the pain your employees will experience when you do. I call them the five "C's" of successful evaluation: consistency, continuity, compliments, criticism, and counsel.

The first thing your subordinates will try to discover is, "what score did the other guy get?" What they are really checking to see is whether or not you were consistent. Employees are very concerned about the boss playing favorites. You'll always like some employees better than others. It's just human nature. But, you must evaluate them in a consistent manner. This means you must have a well-honed system for note taking and documentation. You can't evaluate by the seat of your pants and maintain consistency. There are many evaluation instruments available. If your company has one in place, learn everything there is to know about it. Then apply it consistently across the board.

Most organizations have a formally designated evaluation period, e.g., one year. But, if you are to maintain evaluative continuity, you must informally evaluate much more frequently. This is inconvenient, and it takes time. But you will be much stronger in your position with an underachiever at evaluation time if you have continually reminded him/her of the need to improve performance.

One day, I called in a subordinate who had only been under my supervision for about ten weeks. Her work quality was substandard, and I told her so. She got somewhat defensive, and responded, "Why are you telling me this? It's not evaluation time." I said, "Well, no, it's not report card time yet, but I felt it was time for a progress report. Now you've got some time to bring your grade up." She obviously didn't appreciate my comparison to the grammar school grading system. However, when she saw her evaluation three months later, she was extremely pleased. She had moved from below average performance to just above average. I told her that she should be proud at having made such marked improvement. She said, "Yeah, I guess I didn't appreciate what you were doing when you called me in a few months back. No supervisor has ever done that before. They just hammered me on my formal evaluation, and told me I should have known my work was below average." One of the key principles of evaluative continuity is this: If you do not periodically tell your employees how they are doing, they will assume they are doing fine. It is unfair to keep quiet throughout the whole evaluation period, then slam them with no previous warning.

Compliments are easy to give. All employees like to hear good things. Regardless of how much dirt you have to move, you must find a little bit of gold in each employee. No one likes criticism, but it is more palatable if it is sandwiched in between a couple of complimentary remarks.

Criticism is not so easily delivered. For this reason, it should be offered in a manner that focuses on unacceptable performance, while allowing the employee to save face. If you can't say something good, at least say it in a nice way. Be specific and candid, but avoid judgmental remarks, and be careful with your language. After all, "the first day of spring," and "the last day of a long, nasty winter" may be the same day, but the word combinations do not create the same illusion.

Finally, counseling should always be a part of your evaluative tool kit. Don't tell a subordinate what is wrong, without giving him/her some guidance about how to fix it. Remember, your responsibility is also to train. Write your recommendations for improvement directly into the evaluation narrative. That protects you in case you are required to take more severe action later.

Evaluations make employees nervous, especially if salary increases, bonuses, and merit awards are tied to them. You may not always be able to give them the ratings they desire. But if you follow these guidelines, you will ensure that, like it or not, your subordinates will not be shocked or surprised by your style or their ratings.

What Did He Just Say?

Don't

1) Don't shirk from your responsibility to evaluate properly. Your subordinates deserve an accurate evaluation.

2) Don't wait to criticize and correct poor performance. Help your employees along the way.
3) Don't underestimate the importance of an evaluation. It will follow the employee throughout his/her career.

Do

1) Strive to be consistent in your evaluative technique.
2) Evaluate continually so that his/her formal evaluation scores do not shock the subordinate.
3) Be sure to compliment them in the evaluation narrative.
4) Level criticism fairly and carefully.
5) Give counsel as to how the weak subordinate can improve.

XVI

Another Day, Another Nickel
Understanding Budgets And Financial Controls

Unless you work in a financial environment, your direct interaction with budgets and financial controls will be somewhat limited at the supervisory level. Most organizations relegate money matters to middle and upper management. It is called top down budgeting where management makes the financial decisions and sets the budgeting objectives, while supervisors take on the responsibility for carrying out management's direction.

Some supervisors perceive this to be a disadvantage, citing that the managers who make the decisions and set the directions are not the ones who are tasked to make them work at the operational level.

Others express little concern about financial considerations and prefer to leave budgeting in the hands of upper management, while they concentrate on more operationally based issues.

Regardless, supervisors are regularly impacted by the organization's financial network simply by virtue of their day-to-day activities. The appreciation you will develop for financial responsibility while at the supervisory level will carry over and assist you in the later stages of your management career.

In some respects, a supervisor's role relative to budget and financial controls could best be described as stewardship. When people hear the word "budget," they usually think in terms of dollars. In a larger sense, however, financial control has more global implications than simply revenue. The effectiveness with which your subordinates do their job must also be balanced by efficiency; that is to say, not just doing the right things; but doing them in a cost-efficient, timely manner. An employee who does the job, but takes too much time or wastes resources in the process is not very effective. At this point, the supervisor becomes a major check and balance agent. As the person who reviews time sheets or payroll hours, you become a fiscal officer of first resort to insure that records have been correctly entered and accurately reflect the work activity of your employees. An artificial shift extension here, a few minutes of suspect overtime there, and you have allowed situational ethics to breach the organization's trust, as well as failing in the stewardship of the company resources.

Few employees begin from the outset to cheat the organization. On the other hand, not everyone believes that taking organizational inventory for personal use is wrong. The improper appropriation of a package of paper, a box of paperclips, or a couple of computer discs seems inconsequential when compared to the vast inventory that the company keeps on hand. But experience has taught us that the majority of subordinates who got caught and convicted of company fraud or theft did not begin by stealing large items or amounts.

They started small and just kept comfortably wading until they were in way over their heads.

Once again, it just comes down to paying attention to what is going on around you. If you are insuring that your subordinates do their job without wasting excessive time, you're saving the organization money. If you check to make sure that company issued equipment is not being abused and is in good repair, you are protecting company assets. And if you are always alert to new, more efficient ways of accomplishing the mission, you are acting as a responsible steward of the finances. Remember, you may not directly control the purse strings, but someone, somewhere within the organization does. And those expenses **incurred** by your section are being **charged against** your section. Rest assured that some bean counter in the organization will let your boss know when expenses appear to be out of line.

Working within a budget can be frustrating for supervisors. The financial framework never seems to be sufficient to support all the things that need to be done. Top management is always talking about doing more with less, working smarter not harder, downsizing, and lean budget years. Get used to it. Not one time in twenty-five years did I ever hear the words, "This has been a great year for the organization, so we're going to spend a little more freely during the next fiscal year." That is just not going to happen. Management is always concerned about the bottom line, because ultimately they are held accountable for accomplishing the mission on time and within the budget.

There will always be a scarcity of tangible resources. No matter how big the organization gets, money and supplies will always be limited. And perhaps they should be. I found out many years ago that obtaining more chickens does not necessarily improve the quality of the eggs. It is also a given that, as resources decline, organizational in-fighting becomes more intense. When one organizational group tries to get resources designated for another group, the fur will eventually fly. And here's another little tidbit. The financial power is always concentrated at the top of the organizational pyramid. That's why the big boss is attending a convention in Las Vegas; and you, as a first-level supervisor, can't hire a temporary secretary for a week. The money is there. It's just not available to you.

The inequity will always exist. Two things quickly became very evident to me as a supervisor. One was the golden rule. Not the one in the Bible, but the organizational golden rule...he/she who has the gold rules. The second thing I learned was that budget rules should not be broken. However, if you knew who, or how, then they could be bent in about a million different directions. I'm not talking about unethical compromises here. What I am suggesting is that not everything about organizational budget control is etched in stone. Given that, I realized that there was one group in the organization that could help a poor, struggling supervisor like me more than anyone else. You guessed it—-the fiscal management group. If you can befriend the fiscal control agents, you significantly increase your advantage in the battle for organizational resources.

Soon after I was promoted, I was assigned to one of the executive administrative offices. One of my first tasks was to make arrangements with a local firm to take a formal photograph of the new Police Chief. The first thing I did was to contact the budget office. I asked one of the clerks if money existed for such a photographic session. She assured me that it did. When the photo session was completed, the pictures received, and hung up in the building, I received a bill from the photographer for $800.00, which I forwarded to the fiscal manager. About an hour later, the fiscal manager, whom I had befriended some time back, came to my office with the problem. My mistake was that I never ascertained from the clerk exactly how much money was budgeted for the photography. The budgeted amount was $250.00. I had overspent the budget by $550.00 When the fiscal manager explained this to me, I reached into my briefcase and took out my personal checkbook. He said, "Hey, what are you doing?" I replied, "I have just been promoted. If you think for one minute I'm going to let anyone but you know that my first supervisory decision was a $550.00 mistake, you're crazy." He just smiled. Then he said, "I said there wasn't enough money in the photography account. I never said I couldn't shake a few dollars loose somewhere else." When I asked if it was against the rules, he replied, "Budget rules are bamboo, not oak. You can bend them a great deal without breaking them, PROVIDED you know how." I have no idea how that bill got paid. It just disappeared; and so did the fiscal manager, right after I bought him lunch.

Do not be afraid of budgets and financial controls. They are somewhat alien if you've never been around them. But the more you learn about how they work, their impact on the organization, and who controls them, the more effective you will be in your supervisory position.

What Did He Just Say?

Don't

1) Don't make the mistake of thinking you are not impacted by budgets simply because you are a first-line supervisor. You are very much a part of the budget execution process.
2) Don't let your supervisory control slide relative to financial controls. The organization depends upon you for security.
3) Never expect management to give you a blank check. Resources will always be scarce.

Do

1) Remember that budget rules can be flexed, depending on whom and what you know.
2) Learn all you can about budgeting at your level. It will help later when you actually begin to create budgets and to make large scale financial decisions.
3) Befriend those in the organization who control the purse strings. This is not an ethical compromise. It is simply strategic positioning in the battle for limited resources.

XVII

Would Someone Please Take This Knife Out Of My Back?
Surviving Organizational Politics

There's an old adage that says, "You can't work for an organization for 25 years without feeling at least once in your career that you've been screwed, blued, and tattooed." I certainly know that was true for me. And whether your experience with organizational politics is real or perceived, it is still painful if you are on the receiving end. In fact, that's really the only time it is painful. If you win, it's great. For the uninvolved, organizational politics is somewhat of a spectator sport, where, just like at a tennis match, everyone watches the volleys go back and forth until someone yells, "game, set, match."

In an ideal organizational world, everyone would be rewarded on merit, imbeciles wouldn't rise to positions of power, and success would be defined by talent, hard work, and an occasional lucky break. Unfortunately, such is not the case. Many equate politics to deceit, deception, and self-interest. In some respects they may be correct. But to stop there is both negative and shallow. Politics can also mean gaining power or advantage, controlling people and/or resources, and getting others to do the things you want.

When you enter the ranks of supervisor, you advance to a new level of power and politics. In many respects, this whole primer is about how to shuck and jive your way through the organizational maze and still realize success. It must be possible. Literally thousands of supervisors have done it. But, it requires the skill which comes from factoring yet more elements into your formula for success.

First of all, you must get into the ring and mix it up. When you became a supervisor, you went on the offensive. You put the whole organization on notice that you would accept some additional venerability in order to get off the bench and into the game. Now that you're there, you must play aggressively. That does not necessarily mean getting the other guy before he gets you. What it does mean is that you must realize that no one in your position gets anywhere without playing the political game. And if you're not advancing, you're losing. There is no middle ground. If you are intending to engage in this sport without some skilled political maneuvering, you're a goner. My dad used to say, "Son, if you're gonna pitch, you better learn to catch." Get a book on organizational politics and learn the tactics; not necessarily because you will use all of them, but to learn what may be used against you.

Realize that knowledge is power. If you know something someone else doesn't know, then you have more organizational muscle. I've always said that the most powerful people in the organization are the executive secretaries. They know more than their own bosses know. Why? Because they gather together in the executive washroom every morning, and exchange information they know in order to get the skinny they don't know from the other executive secretaries. Information flies through the organization like poop through a goose. The problem comes from the political spin it acquires as it is passed up, down, and around the communication channels. I have always felt that it was good to be exposed to as much raw information as possible, but to always suspect its validity absent some kind of factual confirmation. Most information is tainted after it has passed through several transmissions. Remember the old kids' game where everyone sits in a circle and the first person whispers in the next person's ear that "the sky is blue," and that person whispers the same thing to the next person. By the time the whispered saying makes the complete circle, "the blue elephant has his trunk in the sky." But even though they get skewed, half-truths can sometimes be useful, and are definitely better than no information at all.

Accept the fact that competition is going to be viscous. On the ball field, competition is healthy. In the organization, it can get downright ugly. There are only so many positions, so many resources, and so much legitimate power to go around. And you can forget sportsmanship. It goes right down the tubes when you're talking about competition for salaries, bonuses, and positioning on the corporate ladder. I have known employees to use lies, threats, intimidation, petitions, lawsuits, back-room deals, begging, unions, payoffs, sex, and religion to gain a step up on the other guy. Talent works too, but talent isn't political. When it comes to competition, you need to keep your eyes open and your antennae up. If you don't, you will get trampled when you least expect it, by someone you would never have suspected. My rule has always been that you should keep your friends close and your enemies closer. And the corollary to that rule is that friends can be enemies in the blink of an eye when it comes to organizational competition.

Watch out for empire builders. Theoretically, management establishes a direction for the organization, and everyone is supposed to strive for the achievement of similar goals. Empire builders, however, put their own political gain above the organization and others. Every decision they make is based upon what will enrich their own chances for advancement. They will say anything, or do anything which exhibits them in a favorable light. They will also abuse their subordinates. They will assign projects, then take full credit with no mention of the people who actually did the work. They will appear to be your friend and confidant, then they'll use the confidential information against you to feather their own nest. I once had a peer supervisor invite me to lunch. She was joining our work group, but had never worked for my boss. Over lunch, she asked some very pointed questions about him, and I was confidentially candid. I told her he was very difficult to work for, and was sometimes unreasonable in his demands. The next day I received the scathing of my professional career. She had gone directly to him behind my back. She told him everything I had said, suggesting to him that she was soooo confused because she had heard nothing but wonderful things about him until I "dumped" on her. Her self-proclaimed reason for going to him was to see if he could clear up the misconceptions I had generated. It wasn't fatal, and he soon saw her for what she was. But it was a gut wrenching way for me to learn about empire builders and the tactics they will employ.

Beware of the lickspittle. It is alive and well. Lickspittles are those fawning, pandering, toady subordinates who want to polish your apple not because of who you are, but because of your rank. These employees are not particularly dangerous, but they will ingratiate themselves in such an obsequious fashion that a careless supervisor will begin to believe the mush they dish out. They always know when you're having a bad day, and they show up with just the right remedy. They compliment you fastidiously and play up to you at every public opportunity. They bring you gifts and look for opportunities to do favors. They watch your mannerisms, then they take on similar characteristics. It's almost as if they're engaging in some form of perverted hero worship. Take care that you see them for what they really are and know that the minute you are no longer their boss, they won't give you the time of day.

Every time I watch kids play double dutch jump rope, I am reminded of organizational politics. Double dutch jump rope requires the jumper to negotiate two ropes which are twirling in opposite directions at the same time. It is a tricky maneuver to avoid being whipped by the ropes, but the jumper who is talented enough can jump in a synchronized, rhythmic motion, avoid both ropes, and have a good time doing it. So many supervisors get discouraged and disenchanted when they realize the tremendous power that politics wields inside the organization. It is influential to be sure. But it should not be your sole concern. Every matador who faces the bull knows the risks involved. Regardless, he enters the ring focused on his objective—to defeat the bull. Your job as a supervisor will inevitably force you into the political arena. Don't be disheartened. Your primary responsibility should be to find that synchronized, rhythmic motion which allows you to avoid being politically whip-sawed, while still managing to have a good time doing your job.

What Did He Just Say?

Don't

1) Don't expect to finish your career without being stung a time or two by organizational politics. It is painful, but seldom fatal.

2) Don't shun the political arena. It is a strategy you must learn to use if you are to be a supervisory survivor.

3) Don't be deceived by the pandering subordinate. They only value your organizational position.

Do

1) Learn as much about organizational politics as you can. It can be a useful ally or a dangerous enemy.

2) Become an information sponge. The more you know, the more powerful you become.

3) Realize the nasty nature of organizational competition. It can turn friends into enemies very quickly.

4) Learn to roll with the political punches. The key is not to avoid organizational politics, but to successfully bob and weave your way through it.

XVIII

How About A Drink After Work?
Ethical Supervision

A supervisor once interviewed me for a new position. Before he asked me any questions, he said to me, "I want you to know at the outset that if you get this position, I am going to take credit for every good thing you do, and you're going to take the blame for every mistake you make. If you can't handle that, you should probably reconsider." Now, I'm not suggesting that his methods were proper, but at least I knew from the beginning how he conducted himself as a supervisor. Most supervisors who play games like that won't admit it, even when they get caught.

The title of supervisor carries with it a level of ethical responsibility. Although you may not be administered an oath like a physician or a police officer, you are still in a position to impact other people. For that reason, there is an expectation that your behavior and your professional activities will be conducted on a higher plane.

Initially, you have a responsibility to learn to do your job well. Most of us can recite horror stories about poor supervisors for whom we have worked. In many cases, it is because the supervisor accepted a promotion, but never invested the time and energy to learn to do the job. If you are reading this primer, then you are off to a good start. But this is just the tip of the iceberg. You owe it to yourself, and the organization that promoted you, to seek supervisory excellence. You should access every possible learning mechanism to improve your supervisory skill. If you make the investment, you'll become one of those supervisors who is admired and respected.

It is also your responsibility to maintain a professional relationship with your subordinates. It is impossible to work side by side each day without developing some degree of affinity. But, the extent to which those relationships progress is, in many respects, under your control. For that reason, prudence and good judgment on your part are mandatory. Your subordinates hear what you say and watch what you do very closely. They may not say a word, but they form some pretty concrete conceptions about you based upon your behavior. Some years ago, one of my peers hosted a Christmas party for everyone who worked in our section. I was out-of-town and unable to attend. When I returned to work, however, I could sense that something was amiss. It didn't take long before I learned the story. Our supervisor had attended the party, absent his wife, and had spent the evening flirting with and groping all of his young subordinates' spouses. Although the subordinates were livid, and the wives appalled, they feared that making a scene might jeopardize their working relationship with the supervisor. As it turned out, the working relationship was irrevocably damaged anyway. Word spread like wild fire, and the supervisor was never able to shake his reputation as a lecher and womanizer.

There is nothing you can do on the job that will justify or compensate for inappropriate behavior around your subordinates outside the workplace. Does that preclude activities such as having a drink together after work? You as the supervisor must decide. French kissing a rattlesnake doesn't always mean you're going to get bit; but if you plan to do it regularly, it would behoove you to learn as much as possible about fangs.

As their supervisor, you have a duty to tend to the needs of your employees. In fact, I have stated earlier that by doing so, you learn personal characteristics that will assist you in your supervisory duties. But, you must also know where that duty ends. Once your employees learn to trust you, they will come to you individually with all sorts of non-work related problems. Remember that you are their supervisor; not their wet nurse, paramour, minister, physician, or psychologist. You have an ethical responsibility not to overstep your boundaries and/or your abilities in an effort to help them through times of trouble. This does not preclude casual conversation, nor does it absolve you of your job to put up with a certain amount of whining. Providing a referral is always acceptable. In most instances, however, it should be your only act of crisis intervention. In a training seminar regarding employee counseling, an instructor summed it up quite nicely when he said, "It's good to help an employee who has a monkey on his/her back, but under no circumstance do you take the monkey."

Finally, you have an ethical responsibility to maintain and nurture an allegiance to your subordinates. You are responsible to see that they do the work. But if they, in fact, do it, you should never hesitate to give them the credit. Anything less is unethical. I was once instructed by my supervisor to redesign our large office space and submit a floor plan for his consideration. When I submitted the plan, he looked it over and said, "Well, this is not exactly what I had in mind. Try it again." Frustrated with such non-specific feedback, I was forced to guess at what he wanted. After several additional tries, he accepted the project, and I heard nothing more. Two months later, at an employee award ceremony, he was awarded a plaque and a certificate for the design plan which I had done. He had simply put his name on the cover, and added an additional page at the end listing me and several others as "technical advisors." The point was not that he got a cheap plaque, and I didn't. The point was that he had taken credit for my work. Perhaps because he was the boss, and had commissioned the project, he felt he could claim ownership. As his subordinate, I saw him as nothing more than a thief. Allegiance to employees ensures them that you will not breach fidelity for personal or professional gain. The first time you do it, you will lose their loyalty for good.

Ethical supervision is not easy. The reason is because it revolves around such lofty concepts as honesty, emotional discipline, and loyalty. You will certainly make errors during your tenure as a supervisor. Procedural mistakes are forgivable and, in most instances, correctable. Ethical mistakes are much more complex, and much less forgiving. Fortunately, you get advanced notice of ethical errors. As one of my mentors put it, "If you didn't know it when you did it, it was probably procedural. If you knew before you did it, and you did it anyway, it was probably ethical." Regardless of your supervisory style, you should strive to master the art of ethical supervision. I have never known a supervisor who wasn't better served by practicing it constantly.

What Did He Just Say?

Don't

1) Don't just accept the promotion. Learn to do your job well. You have an ethical responsibility to do so.
2) Don't compromise your behavior with your employees. There is no way to come back from it.

3) Don't take credit for the work of others. It destroys the allegiance which is necessary for a good supervisor/subordinate relationship.

Do

1) If you have supervisory idiosyncrasies, admit them right up front. Don't force your subordinates to guess.
2) Use your best judgment when considering the type of relationship you want with your subordinates.
3) Realize your limitations when tending to the needs of your subordinates. Refer them to professionals who can help.

XIX

I Must Be Losing My Mind
Handling Supervisory Stress

No one said this was going to be easy. In fact, no one probably said anything, except congratulations. That's the way it generally goes. But it doesn't change the way you feel, and you may be feeling a little insecure at this stage. This is to be expected. You are bound to experience some unique stresses as you settle into your new supervisory responsibility. Take comfort in the fact that it will ameliorate as you become acclimated to the increased amount of responsibility you have incurred. Until then, there are some steps you can take that will help you through this stressful adjustment period.

The first thing you need is a reality check. This is not the kind of job you learn in one week. The term "learning curve" refers to that period of time required to learn something new. It can be longer for some things than others, but simply **wanting** to shorten the curve is not going to make it happen. It is very normal to experience feelings of inadequacy, frustration, and hesitancy during the first few months. Don't worry about it. The fact that you feel the way you do means that you are concerned about doing the job properly. Your knowledge will eventually catch up with your desire to perform well, and coming to work will once again be routine and comfortable.

Secondly, you must learn to leave the job in the workplace. I learned a long time ago that your unfinished work is always waiting for you when you come back. There is always something that needs attention. Routinely taking work home with you will seldom help you catch up, because yet another project will be lying on your desk in the morning. What's more, worrying about work when you're not there increases your stress level to the point that you derive little or no enjoyment from your time away from the job.

Any psychologist will tell you that "escape" is a necessary ingredient to good mental health. Whether that means going to lunch somewhere outside of the office, or playing a computer game for fifteen minutes, the idea is that you mentally leave work and give yourself a chance to recover from the tedious daily grind. Working through lunch, and avoiding breaks is self-defeating. It may seem that you are working harder; but, realistically, you're not getting much more accomplished. Learn to escape occasionally. It will make your working time much more effective.

Developing good peer relationships is important. It gives you an opportunity to vent your frustrations, and it also provides the chance to bounce ideas and questions off of someone in the same working arena. Believe it or not, you are not alone. Other supervisors experience the same problems and are looking for similar solutions. Further, keep your eye out for someone who can serve as a mentor. People love to share their own experiences if you show interest.

Outside of the workplace, there are some additional things you can do to assist you during this transition phase. They may not seem too important, but the key here is to combine a series of individual activities to achieve a cumulative effect.

Both rest and exercise have been shown to have a marked impact on performance in the workplace. It is not unusual for someone who is experiencing significant change to suffer from a lack of proper rest. Bear in mind that rest doesn't necessarily equate to sleep time. If the time spent sleeping is fitful and interspersed with periods of wakefulness and worry, little real rest occurs. Exercise can play a dual role here. Initially, exercise allows you once again to escape from job worries. Because of the way we are made, the mind does not focus on work-related problems while the body in engaged in physical activity. In other words, it is virtually impossible to think about the job if you are putting your physical body through its paces. Secondly, exercise for sufficient periods results in higher energy levels which provide additional support when you are on the job. It also helps you to sleep better, provided it is not done just before bedtime.

There is another type of rest which is always important, but particularly during stressful transitions. It is called emotional rest, and it is accomplished simply by being alone. You will soon discover that a majority of your supervisory time is spent dealing with other people. In order to achieve some sort of balance, you must set aside time for yourself outside the workplace. It does not matter what you do with the time, provided it is enjoyable, non-work related, and solitary. It may seem somewhat selfish, especially if you have a very active family life. However, you will find that the few minutes you spend by yourself will make you much more effective during the periods you spend dealing with others.

After some time has passed, you will need to stop and assess whether or not you have made the appropriate adjustment to your new position. You may be doing a good job at work, but experiencing physical or mental health problems because of it. Keep in touch with close friends and relatives who knew you before you became a supervisor. Query them as to any changes they may have noticed between then and now. Maintain regular medical check-ups to insure that no significant physical problems have developed. Many times, increased stress levels will result in higher blood pressure, increased fatigue, minor aches and pains, and tension headaches.

Change is always traumatic, even if it is for the good. You are bound to experience some consternation as you take on the challenges of your new job. By practicing some of the coping skills described here, you will lessen the impact this change has brought about. Remember, also, that your new subordinates are also experiencing the challenge brought about by a deviation in their comfort zone. The reactions you perceive from them at this point may not be reflective of their long-term responses, once they become comfortable with you.

Time has a way of fixing things. Unfortunately, you cannot hurry it along. Expect that as the days go by, the tasks which are now unfamiliar will become easier, and the people more predictable. Until then, just stay focused on your job responsibilities, and use the above strategies to work through the difficult periods.

What Did He Just Say?

Don't

1) Don't give up. It takes time to work through the learning curve.
2) As a general rule, don't take work home with you. It isn't worth sacrificing your mental health.
3) Don't suffer by yourself. Develop peer relationships which will allow you an outlet for venting and sharing.

Do

1) Start an exercise program, and insure you get a sufficient amount of rest.

2) Set aside some time for yourself. You need the emotional support it provides.

3) Assess your situation after some time has passed. Take whatever steps are necessary to maintain your health.

XX

What's My Next Move?
Preparing For The Next Promotion

It might seem silly to be thinking about further advancement when you're still celebrating your recent promotion. Especially since you'll be in this position for the foreseeable future. But even during the early stages of your supervisory career, you need to ask yourself a number of pertinent questions. For example, do I enjoy having subordinates, and handling the challenges that supervisors face? Do I want to move up to the next level of management, or am I content to be a supervisor for the remainder of my career?

Am I willing to invest the time and energy necessary to prepare for the next step? Will middle management opportunities be available when my time comes? Is a management salary worth the hours and the risks involved?

Everyone's answers will be different. And it may well be that you have no desire whatsoever to advance beyond the position of supervisor. If so, reserve this chapter in case you change your mind in the future. But if you even suspect that you may want to become a middle manager, you must develop a master plan. There are many things which you must accomplish over time, both preparatory and strategic, if you are to be successful.

The most important thing you do to prepare for middle management is to become a good supervisor first. For that reason, you should be firmly ensconced in your supervisory role before directing any effort toward the next step. Besides that, it does not speak well of you politically to evidence interest in the next promotion right away. Learn to be an effective supervisor. You will carry those skills with you no matter how high you climb.

It has been my experience that simply doing your job is not enough to get you promoted to the next level. Competition is too great, and middle management positions are too few. Given that, you must come to the table with better credentials, and an impressive laundry list of activities that will draw the promoter's attention to you.

The most meaningful credential you can display is competence which, in my opinion, is achieved through training. As a supervisor you should seek out and participate in multiple levels of training. General supervisory training involves training such as is provided in this primer. It deals with basic supervisory techniques, and gives you the tools you need to do the overall job well. Once you have the general training under your belt, you should strive for a number of specialized courses which indoctrinate you to the more intricate details of the supervisory function. Courses dealing with finance, communication, business law, organizational behavior, discipline, and motivation are but a few. After you have amassed a significant amount of supervisory training experience, you can then turn your attention to generalized management training. By the time you are eligible for promotion to mid-management, you should be totally familiar with the general functions of the position. All of this equates to a great deal of work. If your organization does not offer some or all of these courses, seek them out at local colleges or professional training companies. Under some circumstances, you may have to finance the course work on your own. If so, offer to pay for the training if your boss will allow you to attend on company time. And save every certificate, regardless of the nature of the training. You may be required to provide evidence of attendance at a later time.

It may be beneficial to join a professional association. These organizations print newsletters, sponsor conferences, and produce training materials that can help you. Besides, active membership in professional associations always looks good on your resume.

Develop a reputation in your organization as someone who is always willing to do more than the minimum. Ask for, and accept membership on organizational committees which will allow you to network with both managers and subordinates. Make yourself available to take on projects that are neither easy nor popular. Take care not to get in over your head, but give management witness that you are the "go to" guy or gal who can get stuff done.

In more recent years, management has encouraged its employees to take an active role in community and/or civic work. If your management team supports this, look around for some opportunity to offer your expertise. It need not be extremely time consuming. But it sends a powerful message that you understand the global nature of voluntary service.

Transfer into positions which give you increased management visibility. Generally speaking, though not always, administrative jobs such as planning, finance, records, and professional standards accomplish this objective nicely. They are not particularly easy, nor fun to do, but management appreciates a supervisor with a diverse background.

And, last but not least, keep your nose clean. Go back and read the chapter on ethical supervision. Although most organizations do not have control over your activities outside the workplace, they will quietly skip over you for promotion if your personal behavior is sullied.

I have had the opportunity to talk with many managers who have reached the top of their individual organizations. Not one of them ever said, "Well, I just hung around, and they kept promoting me until I reached the top." Each one of them had some type of objective-driven plan that helped them get where they wanted to go.

You must do the same. Regardless of how talented you are, neither the world nor the organization will beat a path to your door. You must demonstrate your interest, then back it up with enough evidence to convince management that you want to be a part of their team.

What Did He Just Say?

Don't

1) Don't actually start working on your next promotion until you are well adjusted in your young supervisory role.
2) Don't expect to get your next promotion based on luck. You must develop a promotional plan, then follow it diligently.
3) Don't be satisfied with doing the bare minimum. Look for opportunities to show off your talents.

Do

1) Demonstrate your competence for promotion through constant training.

2) Go after projects which need doing, but are not popular. Show management that you can be depended upon for hard assignments.

3) Be careful of your personal behavior. It can influence management's promotional decisions.

ABOUT THE AUTHOR

Jim Weaver attended the University of Central Florida (B.S.,1972) and Rollins College (M.S., 1977) where he studied management at the prestigious Crummer Graduate School of Business. He teaches supervision, management, and public safety courses at both alma maters as well as numerous other colleges and universities. He served with the Orlando Police Department in Orlando, Florida for 25 years, retiring at the rank of Deputy Chief of Police. He is presently on staff at the Criminal Justice Institute at Valencia Community College. He is the author of numerous articles on the subject of supervision and personnel management

CPSIA information can be obtained
at www.ICGtesting.com
Printed in the USA
LVOW03s2044291017
554206LV00001B/68/P